In Her Soul the Pale Rooms of the Moon Were Wandering

Poems

Also by Toni Thomas:

Chosen
Fast as Lightening
Walking on Water
Blue Halo
Ace Raider of the Unfathomable Universe
You'll be Fast as Lightning Coveting my Painted Tail
Hotsy Totsy Ballroom
Love Adrift in the City of Stars
In the Pink Arms of the City
In the Kingdom of Longing
The Things We Don't Know
In the Boarding House for Unclaimed Girls
They Became Wing Perfect and Flew
Unburdened Kisses
Bandits Come and Remove Her Body in the Night
There is This
Here
The Smooth White Vanishing
Perishing in the Rain
A Different Measure of Moonlight
The Secret Language of River
Inside Her a River of Snow was Traveling

In Her Soul the Pale Rooms of the Moon Were Wandering

Poems

First published in 2024 by Annalese Press
134 Towngate
Netherthong
Holmfirth
West Yorkshire HD9 3XZ
England

Copyright © 2013 Toni Thomas
Published 2024

*All characters and situations appearing
in these pages are creatures of the imagination and in the
service of poetry.
Any resemblance to real persons
living or dead, is purely coincidental.*

All rights reserved. No part of this publication may be reproduced, stored, or transmitted in any form, or by any means electronic, mechanical or photocopying, recording or otherwise, without the express written permission of the publisher.

Cover design and layout by Peter Wadsworth
The Convalescent, Gwen John, circa 1923

British Library Cataloguing-in-Publication Data
A catalogue record for this book is available on request from the British Library.

ISBN 978-1-0685744-0-5

Contents

Part One *We Were Stargazing*

The light can be perilous	3
We were dancing the Torramalino	4
I try to lure you	5
You whisper *forever*	6
The fireflies are flashing	7
Winter	8
You ransom the mirror	9
We were stargazing	10
In winter my life is a snarl	12
Sooth Me, baby	13
After You Say *I am divorcing You*	14
We are *not* talking about departure	16
Did it come easy	17

Part Two *The Cold of Poland*

In my dream	21
It is the season of twined thread	22
I am traveling in a small boat	24
My body	25
At your birthday	26
My daughter tells stories	27

Part Three   *Strangled Kittens*

I live in a room	31
Some things grow opaque	32
You like to yardstick love	33
Is it treason	34
In your drink	35
You are strangling kittens	37
We are traveling in a glass bottom boat	38
I shoulder the yard	39
You wander a siren hotel	40
You sticker your face	41
I am your seeing eye dog	42
You storage locker	43

Part Four   *The Mink of Men's Abject Wanderings*

My children collect	47
It is the year you stop	48
In my dream	49
In one of my past lives	50
Impudent ponies are hard to handle	51
Broken	52
I don't need to say goodbye	53
Back then	54
I make way for new roads	57
Now I stalk the field	58

Part Five   *My Dazzled Winter*

My sister	61
Make me	62
I wore your ring	64
I kept cursing the day	66
When I grew tired	67
How do I explain	68
Joy	70
I stand knee deep in pond water	72
We pocket hope	73
You are lathed grass	74
I show you	75
What if the world drinks quinine	76

With its yellow pears
And wild roses everywhere
The shore hangs in the lake,
O gracious swans,
And drunk with kisses
You dip your heads
In the sobering holy water.

Friedrich Holderlin

Keep some room in your heart
for the unimaginable.

Mary Oliver

Part One

We Were Stargazing

The light can be perilous

stiff as the ivory of sermons
teased hair
tooth picked sandwiches
for the deceased.

We have grown used to
the way it crucifies yard toys
ranunculi, farm workers
drives in a hard stake.

The light can be perilous.
But then so is our love
its croon and careless
way you jab midnight
flirt emails.

In the square a band of boys
chase cats, stink bugs
coax them into cardboard
one by one
pull off their wings.

We are dancing the Torramalino

a mariachi band, bronzed skin
gold braided pants, hectic fingers.
·I spell your name in damp kisses.

You slug merlot
smash your glass on the tile
for good luck you say
spray my canary yellow skirt
in scarlet.

We have barely started to
memorize poems, nurse lips
pronounce *lastness* a four letter word
with no bug bites.

We are dancing the Torramalino.
I twirl and twirl.
You pull me in close as a glued bird.
The ceiling fan waves.

Why wouldn't I believe
in love that lasts
never stymies the dark
with hailstones?

I try to lure you

with bok choy and rice.
Bowls of it.
Swamp with soy sauce
blow kisses that
wander your lips
uncertain as winter.

Your words practice agility
bust over roads
flatten the snow

trivialize peril
as if you have no habit
of deserting things.

You whisper *forever*

its slow soft vows
make me believe in the
return of the cornfield
willingness of our trees
to bear fruit.

After the Schubert, bowls of rice
sliced orange
we sit on the porch
stall the peril of erasure
way you will flirt
axe things

as if at this moment
the last day of March
gazing across the meadow
the elk shaved raspberry stalks
our lips pebbled with Rilke
all things are palpable
decent.

The fireflies are flashing

their autumn farewell
forecast of hard winter.
I want to stay married to eyelet
not pauper the wind's dust field.

You sweep floor
paper the walls with conceit
vagrant women

lean but never come
inside the thigh high
corn field
exuberance of my bed.

Winter

deals in rock salt
snow blinded windows.
You scrap our drive
bald as sin

forget my fleet and frill
offer up skin so thick
the day stops pawing.

When did I start to
believe your words
their combed and petted

begin to propagate winter
thick with thorns?

You ransom the mirror

plaster it with swastikas
a fine combed gaze.

In our field
the tiger lilies drink your forgetful
turn crow talk
cropped women.

A slow child arrives
arm wrestles the wind
watches you suffocate slugs
Hitler your ascension over the roses
curve your lips around
spotless things.

In this child's soul
the pale rooms of the moon
are wandering.

We were stargazing

and somehow in its rarity
I knew it meant the end coming.
The closeness and all
wonder of wonders – Ursula Minor
in the damp distance above the bridge
this welcome fleeting intimacy

you of the sedge feet
who will lead me onto the veranda
studded with limp geranium
and say in plain declarative language
I am divorcing you

and it is like you to do it in this way
after the thin blades of Stilton cheese
the sexy undies
anniversary weekend
after the years of waiting
the endless waiting
secret trysts, lies
private emails

night after night my body pressed
into those silky negligees
waiting for the 3am of you
to travel wine flushed, porn satiated
back into our bed.

We were stargazing a fortnight ago.
You rubbed my feet after the blister
from the Gorge hike.

And I remember in the hall mirror
how you paused to admire your image
flashing back -
50's, academic, newly lean

your sterling mind jostling
behind blue eyes, loose curls.
The sky almost iridescent
under the palsied moon
the Stilton cheese
dinner of pasta and red sauce
cheap merlot still
stalled on our lips.

In winter my life is a snarl

of lunchboxes, slushed roads.
I stoke the parlor fire
grill pancakes
let my children
whittle and charm.

One day when they go off
to big places, leave here behind
will I wonder
where's my love?

Sometimes I worship worn shoes
their lack of strut
way they handhold dirt
keep the carpet from slipping
travel by slow boat
nuzzle lilt, portage, cat hair
castoffs that rub their skin

find a wordless language to
navigate the wind's weeping.

Sooth me, baby

I want to say
as if kisses have their secret
stories to tell
seasons of despair, homecoming
spring pullets
saucy shoes.

Sooth me, baby
how long have I wanted
to stammer more than
the reasonable
coo in your ear
offer up finger food for the dead
toy sheep
chunks of mango
the more not the less of me

find in you the willing door
soft entry?

After You Say *I am Divorcing You*

I field your desertions, private emails
into the baking of bread
slice it merciless
the way you slice words
fairy kingdoms
let the table soot marry the stove
shrink wrap your lips.

See how I lounge in the less
field mice into folded stories
travel my children, the dogs, houseplants
remember my heathen mother
beautiful, insolent in her sloped skirt
how too young she martyred
her cargo of canvases
in the hard mesh of my father's voice

the way she stampeded the snow
that last shrill winter
in flip flops, blue kimono
before her heart splintered.

And I remember the shepherd in my glass ball
wrapped in a muslin cape
the hooded ruse of her, pale and simple
as a friar slipping over the hardened fields

how unperturbed she opens her Eskimo hands
crosses over into the white of my soul

and I think back to my children this afternoon
the way they cut paper into intricate flakes
pinned them onto the window
searched the yard
in the hope of snow.

We are *not* talking about departure

the lost grain
house for sale on a stick
fair-thee-wells
storage unit that will eat up
my books, negligees
spoon sets, shampoo
turn our room into parched plants
not talking about the way
your voice cargoes winter
how in the future I will never again
compost these fields

about how perfunctory
smiley we must be
stick pinned in place
asked not to squirm.

We are *not* talking about the way
I will be exiled into an apartment
asked to license your desertions
hang them out to dry
watch you perfume the air
sweet talk relatives, strangers
attractive women.

We are not talking about
the triumph of bat wings
way you carve your fate into
a card hand loaded with aces
ruby red as a girl's busted heart.

Did it come easy

to walk away
exile me
from the weight of your blades?

Can you believe I loved you
full, close and even in the end
maybe still would have married you.
Can you believe we had a family
a boy child, daughter
lauded them with forest, meadow
paint pots, birthday parties
blue fairies.

Can you believe there was a home
just a stone's throw from the river
that took in the view, bald eagles
raised beds
raspberry vines, forsythia
a single plum tree.

Can you believe the first time
you courted me with a milk jug of daisies
that it was sometimes a good life
godly even -
whatever your mind fought in it -
that love for closeness you couldn't bear.

Can you believe someone would want to
break it in half, sever it
watch the parts bleed.

I can believe it. And you did.
You did.

PART TWO

The Cold of Poland

In my dream

we dish out soup
peopled with fat noodles.
I am more than a calendar pin up
girl in a clashing red sweater
who disbars the rain.

We eat snow
grow a shimmer pond
harbor of honey.
Mythic deer forage.
The day is enough.

In my dream
carp leap off the face
of our plates
potatoes twirl
I offer up card tricks
a kiss party
bring you back
eager
bluesy
to my bed.

It is the season of twined thread

honey coated throat lozenges
mac and cheese, dessert cake
the season of stenciled glass
thick kitty slippers
life on a pole stick
the assault of abbreviated light
before thawed April saves.

It is the season of penny candies
a blue arcade
thick soup crammed with potato
the sickly tyrant of love
that slips into my bed sheets
pretends a denouement of winter
then trundles away.

It is the season of corded wood
a moss speckled roof
deadfall and road kill
one thin band of deer foraging.

I had tasted hope
that thrifty cousin of despair
tasted silence
knew what it was to be petted
like a docile animal
tied to formica, do lists

had tasted your lips
the ones that are always traveling
by freight train

bound for other places
anxious for the next and the next.

It is the season of colored thread
dogs reconciled to the rag rug
the rupture of studded snows
knife blades
emails from late night coo girls
divorce papers
the shitload of bills
children who aren't saying

the tyranny of night angels
who refuse to lift winged
as fruit bats
from the torn flecked
wordless soup of my voice.

I am traveling in a small boat

grey as the skin of whales
want to sticker your life
plaster the lies out
keep faith

want to recite Neruda
sing my life
as a homage to small ends
your fled imperialism.

It is painful watching you
manhandle the fig trees
squeeze our harvest
into your arm's thick forest

be the pretend prince
who never breaks a nose
sidles his academic days
with pearled elocution
blue carrion.

My body

sits in the empty room
of a foreign city
speaks the guttural language
of summer birds weeping.

A morgue grows thick in the center
smells of attrition, exiled dogs
sullen children
boxed toys
expensive attorneys.

Sometimes the card playing
painted plates
photographs, wish list
won't save
nor the bowls of stir-about
the no place to go
endless paw of silk stockings.

I watch the house shrink into
plastic wrapped eggs, burnt toast
plates of cheese sandwich
half-eaten on the side table.

See how your words traitor
flirt their way into other fields
feed on derision
devour the best of the fruit
we once laid.

At your birthday

you drink wine
rivers of it, grow tipsy
sport a crimson tongue
smooth words that
clog the loudspeaker.

I am quartered into lemon
elbowed by ice fields
spiked thistle
but meadows of shy deer
vow to grow back in me.

Your cake looks crowded
holds fifty candles.
It is hard to get them to fit.

You blow, made a wish, blow again
till the waxed bodies
sit with extinguished flame
and out of your mouth's cramped suitcase
come a host of dark birds.

I once confused them with home.

My daughter tells stories

thick robed, sprinkled with rabbits
a princess, lapdogs
horses with manes the texture of corn silk.
Her lamplight, the hearth fire
burn with enviable light.

My daughter tells stories, not about
her four years in a Chinese orphanage
but peopled with elk, possum, deer
that forage the neighbor's orchard.
They do not speak of beheading
the queen's lost child
giant who devours tree limbs
do not speak of broken marriages
a windowless room
mother who gets dysentery
the way a girl's treasure can get boxed
emptied fast as her heart
whole tribes vanish from famine
winter's starved wolves.

My daughter insists on spaniels
a maypole, frogs leaping
that every green wish stays cupped
in the snug of her soul's meadow.

PART THREE

Strangled Kittens

I live in a room

of exiled puppets
they mumble *unfair*
don't like the cold of Poland
entering.

You slip into snowshoes
build a new home
call it your sheltering meadow
crowd the dark with other names.

The puppets
their green kingdom
loose limbs
frolicsome lovemaking
buried
without regret.

Some things grow opaque

become a muddied road
hard candy
cross between attack dog
and tainted schoolboy.

Some lovers turn faithless
grease words
glass jar panties

nurse pyrotechnics
cripple the wind for asking.

You like to yardstick love

knock the plush out of god calling
sacrifice the limbs of roses
in the name of future.

See how I siphon the lies
out of your side table
no longer let you force feed

see how I attempt to spin
in my shy excess
turn your spiny wants
into a moon flecked version
of winter.

Is it treason

the way you fine comb wings
tease then stonewall
expatriate the bedroom
straight pin the voice of god
to our desiccated fruit trees

buy a tidy roof rack
lycra shorts
new kayak, Viagra

make every feathered
open estuary
next in line
your prey?

In your drink

were Spanish olives
speared on a stick
as if you collect things
dark skirts, green rind
sparkling water
flush them down
your mouth's blue toilet
listen to the audible scream
death brings.

But did you memorize their contours
wet dreams, love notes
Castilian sunset
cicada singing across the torn field?

Did they squirm before you
married them to your throat?
Was your lust honest
did you really notice their feelings
slinky nightdress
desire to dance the tarantella
beyond the edgy blade of your toothpick?

They were Spanish olives
not prone to preciousness
a hidden gun

stabbed one by one
then tossed into tall tingly glasses.

Some of them were mothers of small children.
It hadn't occurred to you that it mattered.
You staked them on wood sticks
sucked out the brine
grew territorial over the tall glasses
the way some men grow territorial
over the barbed of their beds.

It is the year of the busted summer.
The truant black rustle of bird wings.
The year of false smiles and divorce papers
where every serene evening starts
and ends with a prick.

You are strangling kittens

a play game of sorts
squeeze till they squeal
spilt milk on the linoleum
a perforated past.

I have never liked hybrid words
that slick down a hailstorm
talc the hands white.
Afterwards an aerosoled room
your parted in the middle profile.

On the porch boxed shoes, coats
an erector set, dollhouse
tricycles, paper hearts and detritus.
The U-Haul truck about to arrive.

Is it triumphant
to commit adultery
hold an animal by the throat
watch her beg for mercy
as you squeeze?

We are traveling in a glass bottom boat

ample in its width and gaze.
You complain the seats are cramped
crowd your voice
your body thick as a heat wave

at night run a brothel
for unschooled girls
come with pills
unzip your pants
as if paradise is calling.
They are young
may someday tell on you.

We are traveling in a boat
with a glass bottom
that illuminates the sea
speckled fish, barnacles, sea urchin.
The seats are squishy.
I want to make love
suck liquid mango from the same straw.

In the brothel
you calculate panties
shrink the past
press white sand, a pint sized boat
calculated seascape
into your blue bottle

watch it stare back
love you senseless
never escape the glass limit
of your gaze.

I shoulder the yard

with a circling pit-bull
am not sure of his trustworthy
the oracular nature of his barks
way he squirms
never apologizes
for the soft bellied toys
he trashes.

I shoulder the yard
with a restless pit-bull.
Watch his sharp teeth
crucify daisies
my colored pinwheel

jab to death what he
pretends to love.

You wander a siren hotel

defamed by the city.
It holds ornate cornices, cigar smoke
cheap mists of cologne
women who call girl their love
for a handful of bills will
listen to your dark calling.

You order up steak, French cigarettes
honey pressed words
pencil my name in your squat notebook
but I am more than *temptress*
more than a powdered envelope
poacher's finger ring
dialect of suburban houses
petted voice.

You marry the hotel's blunt toys
whips and ropes
handcuffs, guillotine
plastic pistols
demand every woman beg for a kiss
sidestep the steely blue denouement
of your gaze.

All night I map your voice
its mascaraed midnight
watch you hostage toys
memorize botany
mount dead butterflies on velvet.

You sticker your face

to the mirror
turn a dry eyed sneer at my weepy
wear love in your trench coat
like a stick bat.

How long does the heart wait
on its shrunken axis
believe miracles can
cross a threshold
melt the cold?

I am your seeing eye dog

but you don't know that
screw with winter
reduce me to the no variety
20 lb. bag of dog kibble
stay up late night
empire the distant stars for your cruise ship.
We have been circling for a long time.

You instruct me in tricks
how to bark on command
stay silent when your finger waves
rollover, lay down
reward with midget dog chews.

I am your seeing eye dog
the one who can lead you out of the forest
abandoned rail station
call out the moon
find the bone buried in a half trashed yard.

You count on my loyalty
the way I sidle neglect
drink the night's blind milk
offer up persistent love notes
am willing to be the fool
wipe up road kill, prissy cats.

I am your seeing eye dog
but you don't know that
debunk scenery
seeing eye dogs
rev your engine
and race.

You storage locker

my books
tarnished flatware
shampoo, socks
till the rain lives in my panties
a drowned gull.

But come April
the bees lift out of their sleep
remember the surplus of me
this thick yellow nectar
I have saved.

Part Four

The Mink of Men's Abject Wanderings

My children collect

plush bears, rabbits
let them roam the wide meadow of their room
tuck a jungle inside their bed sheets.
They are six and three
too young yet to want to cage things.

I wear midnight across a cramped diaspora
wait on the legitimacy of roses
want to become an invitation for animals pawing.

One day god arrives in my forest unperturbed
more than a basalt of dry licks
blue mortuary

and I am no longer afraid
you will devour me.

It is the year you stop wanting to be married to me

stop making believe
and all the negligees, love poems
become has-beens.

I bake bread
mire in debt, attorney fees
attempt to become the knife
with no serrated edge
stay arm's length
no longer fry your eggs
watch you exclamation mark your needs
with a briefcase of Viagra.

See how I practice loss
the shrunken tariff of things
listen to finch slander the tree
with the length of their joy

see how I begin to befriend silence
blaze my steamy hips
unperturbed over the flat din
of your voice's blue faucet.

In my dream

we are in a memorial
but not the bronze of monuments
sticky sweet of nuptial icing
the peril of blued lips
club sandwiches for the deceased.

In my dream you search water.
I carry buckets
a houseboat
watch the fish travel in families.
They hold the color of spilt orange
grazed sunset.

My mother hires a boatman
to take us to Naples.

In my dream I bring fresh water
the canal of my body holds salt
I know how to travel the length of your waves.

In my dream you have no eye for vengeance
celebrate anniversaries
arrive in a white gown, blank name tag
fumble your way to the beach.
I am your seeing eye dog
offer up one of my paws.

The sun doesn't need to act smart
enshrine its voice in gold leaf
reminds me of April, blue gentian
the bright speckled eggs
I have saved.

In one of my past lives

surely I married you
learned your wish list
the blades of your thistle
knew my way around your body
leaned into your pitch and prize
pelleted words, beehive.

In one of my past lives
you colluded with my loose epistles
sucked nectar from blue lips
learned not to run away

became the refrain
of walled peonies
thawed autumn
leaned into the bright umber
of my gaze.

Impudent ponies are hard to handle

balk at the prospect
of aged oats, mud born apples
cleave to their will
deny the clemency of being combed silly.

Now I live in a Shropshire barn
devoid of horses
am not sure I can afford their care
the way they crew-cut my kisses
ask for more than a decent
quotient of sugar cubes.

Some ponies are hard to handle
turn insolent
vandalize bluebells
pummel the best of your daisies.

Broken

You bug jar kisses
arrive at the tawdry decision
to divorce me
girlfriend the woman you have
flaunted like pert enamel.

I go around puddled chartreuse
with my borders broken
want to sweet talk winter
don't know how

move on
begin to nurse
the moon's wet lips
shy forgotten seed
that is left in me.

I don't need to say goodbye

bury you in talc
the fiction of love notes
make believe the handsome
of your words
stand for anything

are more than a soap box derby
bullet proof train
that catalogs want
till even the birds, clouds
earnest sunset
escape

and you are left with only your
loyal picture of flawed women
abject winter.

Back then

we grew pattypan squash
big as melon
netted the raspberries
so elk wouldn't scavenge
collected wormed apples
pulped them into jars of sauce
left the fallen ones
for the deer's supper plate.

I pressed marionberries
into your mouth's damp wing
nursed nasturtium
beside the porch swing.

Were you decent back then —
almost in love with me
willing to notice the swallows
trellised to my hair
worn down chalices

was I more than anonymous
more than the occasional interest
did you always run away
from my kiss and coo
mark time provisional
make me the aberrant child
emotional antidote
for whom all days are days of denial?

Did you ever miss my camisoles, lace slip
grow weary in the solitary rooms
of your porn flecked wintering?

Did I always settle for the armed distance
settle for the way our teenage son mimics disdain
like you finds me incompetent, too emotional
robs me of my brain, filial hand over the rosebuds
did I always turn the other cheek
practice hat tricks
get derided in cards, board games
merely because I was winning, was it in goodwill
you coaxed the children to topple me
or was it your own irresistible urge to crush

did you ever watch the snowy plover marry
her perch in the oak tree
taste the rain drizzle
find the words of my blue pen
more than barely agreeable
more than just a reason to work harder, do better
prostrate the wind?

There is a cruel eye
that grey envelopes poppies
likes to watch their fade and collapse
the tragedy of broken things
people pummeled for their lack of desire
to hold the world tight and squeeze
spend all their might here.

Are there stations of the heart that succor
rather than batter us
girls left free to willow and wind
gifters of apricots
who must sing as if their life depends on it
who ask to be prized not for the curve

of their legs or accomplishments
but for their inborn light
the way they grow quiet
deferential in the trees
drink death down

let god homage their messy woods
the light's afternoon epistles
gather them up
soft?

I make way for new roads

the stain of green light
ornate snow
no treacherous meadow.

All night I drink
the trees' resin
practice bird language
walk the dark
in petal shoes.

Morning arrives
wants to pin last night's moon
to my gaze.
I do not refuse.

Now I stalk the field

bless fate
let the pine tree's wet fur
bend me
puddle my body in the sky's
least saccharine homilies.

The day refuses to stir stick
poke an eye out
renames black spot on the roses
the scarred boy who baits cats
renames my once love
his buffed lips
blue café.

I want to become the carp
so willing
her body turns clear as the river
guileless as spring.

Part Five

My Dazzled Winter

My sister

deals in pencil thin iris
tunneled possum
the yard path's hard dirt
men who like to concrete
squeeze light into a knife blade

arrives in a gauzy skirt
mud infested
makes me vow not to plagiarize
let the past speak dirty.

My sister drizzles
purple onto the green
nubs of crocus
keeps my buds from forsaking
the wet risen lips of the grass.

Make me

an algorithm of your disasters
till I can see my way out the other side
pin me tough and fast and strict
dungareed to the hard hitting sun
of your clothesline
feed me your lies, swamp grass
dwarfed apples

quantum leap my abundance
whittle it into pale sticks
keep turning, turning away
take my hands and stomp
mud coat the frill of my yard daisies

let the imperialism of your voice
crowd the room, erase apostrophes
turn the moon divisive
impel me to suck the heavy tread
of your boots
semester of smug boys stalking

assassinate the house parts
play swing, love notes
pale sheep in my yard
label them *spineless casualties of the dark*
hand tool your rhetoric

gold stipple it
let your fierce travel an empire

but in the final count
watch how I mount my sepulcher
find a voice that supplants rag hills
mount your nights of cruel wandering
never fully drown
watch how I rise up flame proof
beyond your wake.

I wore your ring

small, intricate
its thin gold band, tourmaline
that lapped the sky
clear, unperturbed
let all things in
didn't drown them.

The setting was 19th century
a replica made for the museum store
a season of maypoles, nosegays
men with bluesy lips
girls unhampered by lavender.
It could have been promised for a prom
my first dance, Juliet dress
meadows of abject wandering.

Your clothes were buffed
matched your mental brilliance.
You sang *The Lass of Donegal*
with a practiced voice
hinted of ex-lovers, culled rooms
flowers for the deceased.

I wore your slim gold ring
with the blue stone
like a songstress

new language for love
flamed room calling.

Now I conjure snow
unearth a stubby throne
practice abstinence
travel with the blue blue blue
of the sky's penitential longing
those broken rooms
you have mapped in me.

I kept cursing the day

but still it wanted to marry me
towel dry my hair
couch me in peony
a spindle crib, eyelet.

Over time I have quit drinking quinine
reordered my camisoles
the guttural denouement of rain

welcomed home
my tart and stammer
snowfield
inborn fluencies

learned to mother disaster
turn surly men into the
Sweet William of my bed.

When I grew tired

of rehearsing your road kill
tired of red eye and come cries
god began to spoon-feed new wings.

I marvel at their feathered duff
the way they deflect winter
wear the night loose
launch off chairs, the sloped tree
shed roof
elevated building with a roof deck
summer table for card playing

venture onto your lips
travel their pale grey nonsense
with the language of finch
rain's thunder

no more crammed down my throat
just the sumptuous flap
of spring burning.

How do I explain

this desire so deep, so crazy
full of berm and thistle
candle and calamine
it escapes the banks of the river
flows forceful
even now toward the sea

explain how love moves
beyond the blocked dam
pulverized trees
weeps over our distances
knows the past can't harm
nor airtight words
spewed epitaphs
the way your heart squeezed
my breath
like a snake that devours whole
the body of the road kill

how do I explain
understand from love to love
the way life holds a blue gaze
birds stall in the field

my words hang
unrobed by midnight

the way lovers still keep the memory
of each other's arms
as if god ensures even beyond trespass
a deathbed
there remains the width
of the trees' embrace
forgiveness?

Joy

you celebrate the worn down quotient in things
the tar and tourmaline
stickpins and sagebrush
see into the man dissolved with rain
the heart's painted ponies
into the child sueting bread
for her lunchbox's brave homily

see into words
the longing of shy things
fledgling jonquil
holes that perforate the face of my lover's shoes.

You live in the broken epistles
boarded up house with its roof tilted
lounge in the space beyond curtains
in two by fours, toy pistols, frog slippers
untimely foreclosure
inside polar watches, poorboy sandwiches
the brio and brawn, my father's bald head
my mother's dead voice lifting.

You see inside brothels
the broken down thrum of our longing
the moon's sodden voice
devotion of field grass
the way lovers come back to us

not perfect or gashed midnight
but slow spun

the way the earth, the day
refuses to be pocked to death with a sharp stick
answers us with no remorse
with spring.

I stand knee deep in pond water

watch the first of April's frogs
practice worship
lounge in the boggy
loyal to the bulbous wet
bowl of their lips.

They don't pauper the day
obsess over beauty
need to turn conventionally handsome

remain weed bound
thrush inspired
purveyors of sludge
pond fronds, catkins
the moon's speckled voice.

We pocket hope

shiny as a silver salver
stalled wind
that never shoplifts
grows tyranny
over the bed sheets.

You call back finch
hyacinth, the stone bridge
plant your blanket by the river
let guppies travel my blue equator.

I slice gherkins, pecan cheese
pumpernickel
no longer take *no* for an answer
stroke your cheek
body's pooled estuary

as if deathless summer
has arrived.

You are lathed grass

leap years
the loose skin of frogs
excess of lavender shoes
fretless Abigails

dig out my best voice
aria the sky into swaying
till I don't want to dissect
grow back green foam
float over the house flames

tack a new meadow onto my mirror
ribbon my body
into a bright corsage
invitation to go summering.

I show you

my board games
German doll
miniature tea service

slide in and out of your polar fleece
with my panties, lace bra
storybook the remnant
of last season's corn field.

My love, you are more than
a harsh flashlight
queen bee in a glass dome.
I lick the bounty
the sure of you
your hive's blue resin
honeyed paws.

What if the world drinks quinine

but I refuse to enter
refuse to disown the extravagance of roses
see our lives as less than the loss
of an ancient tune playing

what if my love is more than souiled cinquefoil
chaste dungarees on a taut clothesline
and we are being paraded as soldiers
but the disguise never fit?

And what can I say about the boy
who blindfolds his past
howls at the dark
in the form of indenture

how I want to dig you up
from a robber's grave
find a wordless day, marry it?

What if we are more than our pay stub
house parts, face paint
catalog of needs
the earth offers up an intricate filigree
squats to make room
for our grandest picnic

come now
would I be so strict
to turn away such lamplight
even in the rain?

Toni Thomas lives in Portland, Oregon. Her poems have been published in Austria, Spain, New Zealand, Canada, England, Scotland, and Australia. In the United States her work has appeared in over fifty literary magazines including *Prairie Schooner, North Dakota Quarterly, Hayden's Ferry Review, the Minnesota Review, Notre Dame Review, Poetry East,* and more. She has been twice nominated for a Pushcart prize, and won several awards. She has published twenty-two collections of poetry and six books for children.

Her figurative clay sculptures have been shown in gallery exhibits in Portland and Chicago, displayed in literary magazines, and housed in private collections in the U.S. and England.

Her short documentary *One of Us* was shown at the Trans-ideology: Nostalgia festival in Berlin and at the Museum of Contemporary Art in Taipei.

Since Toni loves to create and sits buried in reams of poems, manuscripts, clay figures and images....she likes to imagine all of them out in the world swaying wild as the lupine.

tonithomaspoetry.com

www.ingramcontent.com/pod-product-compliance
Lightning Source LLC
Chambersburg PA
CBHW030455010526
44118CB00011B/953